THE RED THREAD

Camp Kieve
– 2006 –

THE RED THREAD

Poems

Elizabeth Gordon McKim

→ (elder flower child) and Katy and Tamara

To Erik

With wonder/full memories of our time together in the enchanted Forest –

love elizabeth (elder flower child)

Leapfrog Press
Wellfleet, Massachusetts

Published in 2003 in the United States by
The Leapfrog Press
P.O. Box 1495
95 Commercial Street
Wellfleet, MA 02667-1495, USA
www.leapfrogpress.com

Distributed in the United States by
Consortium Book Sales and Distribution
St. Paul, Minnesota 55114
www.cbsd.com

First Edition

Library of Congress Cataloging-in-Publication Data

McKim, Elizabeth.
 The red thread : poems / by Elizabeth Gordon McKim.-- 1st ed.
   p. cm.
 ISBN 0-9679520-9-3
 I. Title.
 PS3563.A3168R43 2003
 811'.54--dc21

                                                2002155638

For my Daughter:
Jenifer Belknap McKim
My Son-in-Law:
James Joseph Jepsen
And
My Granddaughter:
Chloe Elizabeth Jepsen
And Those Who Come:
After

Acknowledgments

Various poems in this collection originally appeared in the following publications: *Body India* (Yellow Moon Press); *Beyond Words* (Talking Stone Press); *Blue Sofa Review*, *Café Review*, *Poiesis*, *Painted Bride Quarterly*, *Worcester Review*, *Women of Power*, *Create*, *River Styx*; VOX POP: Polyphonic Poetry and Musical Ecstasy (CD).

CONTENTS

Passion's red thread is infinite
Like the earth always under me

Ikkyu
(15th century Zen mystic)

DAWN RAGA

THIS ONE GOES OUT TO:

You
Sitting on the scratchy mat
Gobbling the distinctive cheese
You not talking my language
Just those garbled preverbal sounds
Yes you
Not willing to meet me halfway
Not sharing the secret of my life
Not handing me my nugget
Not giving me my deserved portion of the gold
Not going out in the field with me
Not taking the field trip not holding my umbrella
Not telling me how you did the magic trick
Not taking me to the middle of the double rainbow
Not having a commingling round about midnight
Not having a cappuccino snuggled in the corner of my favorite cafe
Oh how dare you sullen struggler you mooncow
You unruly forget about it
How can I take you anywhere
When you refuse to behave like a grownup
Coming in always with your socks full of holes
When you give me no choice but to leave you alone
Don't you know I have felt you huddled with all the bewildered
Forgotten ones the nameless homeless ones
Don't you think I've heard you out in the hurricane
Tap tapping in the night
Trying to come home without your keys

Trying to find the dilapidated dwelling that has disappeared
Like a puddle in the sun
I heard you throwing curses at me and all the salt soaked sailors
Darkening my dawn when all I wanted
Was a leisurely cruise on a pleasure boat
You shipwreck
You impossible storm heading for disaster
I saw what you did deliberately with the chocolate pudding
Missing your mouth again and again
At that well set table of pundits and programmers
You ruin don't you know
They thought you had suffered a stroke
So now I'm begging you to come out coyote
Let me see you dare I say let me love you
You fine creature in your birthday suit
Rolling down the corridors pushing away the envelope
Forget about your fine grades your fine program your fine
Big picture your fine gold star accomplishments
I like you all grumpy and pointed and ready for a tussle
Your dukes up and your head cocked my dear one my darling
All I ever wanted was to hold you
And know you for my own.

DAWN RAGA

The woman discovers dawn
in the cup of its breaking,
Breaking a fire breathing
Into the sky a siren,
A chant, and even now
She knows where she is growing,
Growing
she has always known
The river opens to her,
The dawn in/side breaking,
Drawn to the fact of her waking
In the cup of her knowing
And she bears with the breaking
Which dawn covers down/river remaking
She moves to the fact of her waking
quickly down in the breath
Of her making
the sound of dawn down-
River re/making, the sift and silt
of her waking the sun on her back
She walks with the motion of turning
the spilling of sun in its quaking,
the spreading of daylight

the gift, the gift, the gift of the morning!

DIRECTIONS

Hold
it. Warm
it with your own life.
Listen to its near and far
pulse. The sounds. The messages.
Find out where it was born.
The year. The time. And who
was there and why. Find out the nature
of its fear. What cave or cliff or curve
of tide has touched it tended it
mended it. Find out what
losses it's sustained
what endings
it has suffered through
what midnight tune it listens to
find out what mother tongue has touched
and tasted it find out what it can know of parents
what song and language it was taught
and if it has a friend an enemy
a tribe a family
what stains and bruises
marks and cracks distinguish it
what surface opens to the air
what inside heart is hiding there
and learn the way it lives
and breathes the fire it knows
and how it moves upon
this earth.

FINDING OUR SHAPES

In any old manner/ we sprawl and stammer/ we move
In bumptious motion/ we don't know what to do about the commotion/
Or how we dare assume our shapes/ we fold our pitiful wings/ we don't know how
To pause/or come to full stop/ we babble/we flail about in the universe/
We clear our throats forever/it seems we have no skin/everything hurts/
We only remember the mud/where we were born/we pretend
Indifference to the mist/ we weep uncontrollably/
We tell a joke/forget the punchline/we aren't prepared for the forest/
We never learned to fight/we want to speak eloquently
At the feast/we have no words/it was the same at the funeral/
We want to declare love/we don't know the first thing about courtship/
We blush/inside we are slow/we always fall apart in a rush/
What comes is impossible/ we say our prayers and poems dumbly/
Same for the lullabies/ red thread ahead
We swerve into blazing

YOU LOOKED AT ME
AND SPOKE SO CLEARLY

Compañero de la vida says to me sweetheart
there is no end and no beginning to this busyness
motion/commotion/lifing/poeting/there is no end
it just keeps on going /on and on/forever and ever
ah men and women/why/every little thing including me
just keeps on keepin' on/forever and ever/I am still
traveling out into the cosmos /believe it/ into
particles of space and light/ into the night/ into
the daze/ahmen and women/into the cornfields into
radical bodegas /into the flatiron/pawnshops into
the Memphis poolrooms /into my heart/lapping your
shores/leaping/into the worn air hovering above the earth
tired and panting/still breathing/into damp babies
newly arrived/into the tired feet of workers/into
the kernel bursting the orange/into blossom/into bet
into sun/into blue screen/strange scream of life

BLAME IT ON

the shaman who flung
50 lbs. of precious jade
into the foaming

mouth of the river
and in his longing prayed
all night and day for love.

Blame it on coyote
climbing the fragile trellis
to the moon – he's gone!

Blame it on the woman
and her slow art as she slowly
combs her silver hair.

Blame it on the man
at the crossroads lost or found
Blame it on the air.

HAVING COME THIS FAR

HAVING COME THIS FAR

always has to go further.
That is how she got her name.
Having Come This Far marks time
by where she has been, where she is,
where she will travel. Her heart
is marked with this traveling,
this light under the log, this shadow
on the red-clay earth, this quick
motion cross a cry-streaked sky.
Having Come This Far hums
and ponders these travelings,
smiles at where she has been,
where she may sleep tonight,
the song tomorrow sings in her dreams,

Having Come This Far has a hat
with many ribbons which she takes
on and off, on and off, as if it belongs to her,
but in fact, she knows deeply,
it is only on loan.

HAVING COME BY FIRE

The summer ferns are taller
the gulls shriller
the sun warmer
the wood-sleek table smoother
the seals down-dipping deeper,
the flames hotter
                    and more cruel.

Having come this far
way past mid-summer, now into
late summer
                              young brown faces
stare out of the globe each day wearing jail sentences
while drugs drop deep
into the neighborhoods.

Screams do no good
Malcolm and Martin dead and gone
boat of the dream sailing into storm
round sea-speckled stones re/mending
reminding me again and again
of home/torn apart
blood in the gutter
outraged birds and damaged nests
                              mothers hunting
for recognizable remnants among rubble

HAVING COME THIS FAR
HAS HIT THE HOT COUNTRY

For Jenifer in Puerto Rico

Having Come This Far has hit the hot country
now and she takes to it:
the red tropical flowers get her every time:
the four o' clock wiltdown, the sea behind her eyes,
the balcony's wrought iron invitations,
the parrot's disheveled kvetch, bars open all night.
The woman's red heels tick blue cobbles on old Spanish ballast
trembling the green splurge of leaves, setting off
the coqui's crazy hinge the way the waves urge her on
and on to level all the old resistances.
She wears no outerwear *Having Come This Far*
cries when she thinks of home: those blank mountains the ache
at the back of the neck ice clanking *Having Come This Far* wants
no part of that old breaking country worn and bleak,
full of remorse and skidding, buried cars,
unshoveled parking places no kidding
Having Come This Far is ready to pack it up and
disappear somewhere deep into the warm country into the azure into
the wet red flowering the green shedding of mufflers
the long overdue warm call of undoing
the wooing.

HAVING COME THIS FAR PASSING ON

Has to go further further than even she remembered
   or dreamt in the dreamtime
      passed sage passed pignon past the widest
         sky her compañero de la vida calls the bucket of blue
           past adobe past mister past noon past arroyo past sorrow passed
              sister passed streets passed coyote grinning ear to trickster ear
passed four directions passed nighttime passed bear passed eagle
   passed death and its driving passed danger and weathers
      passed fur and wild feathers past fetish
         passed dancing past dread its arriving
           past tears past breath and its bearing past
eth past edge past ether past ridge past either
   passed ore past bridge

   now/ow/oh/no/one/won

past breath/past bet/past beth/past ee
   past liza/past knight/past love
      past lore/past now/past elizabetheridge
   past howling and crying/past sighing
      and stealing/past mister/past mercy/past reeling
   past k/past song and its stinging
      past reeling/past midnight and keening
past light/and its passing/past knight
   and his riding toward freedom
      his striding toward stretching our reaching with feeling
         our seeking toward freedom/toward freedom

HAVING CHECKPOINT

Having come this far
she's crossing checkpoints
in the flood of dawn
At noon she bolts
through bullets
in the flames of the frontier

At midnight
Can you hear her
At the border dodging fire
She's crying help
Who can help

Having come home she can not find her home
Her family's flown the coop and gone to the camps
They said they'd be back in a shake
But in fact it's been 3 generations
She's more than vexed

Her brother has 5 bullet wounds lodged above his heart
securely in his shoulders
Her older sister needs 6 hours to get to work
And 6 hours back
counting the interrogation at the checkpoint
Her younger brother's only a boy
She thought that he was going to the school
But he was going to the streets

He's learning names
Like stone and gun and bomb 1 beat
and martyr and revenge 2 beats
like suicide that's 3 and intifada 4
he's learning names
She howls unfair in the wind
And no one whistles back
And there is nothing here
But the other's house
built on the terrible rubble of the other's own
insistent history
Built upon the rubble that was once
Her room her mother's and her father's rooms
The kitchen where they made tabouli with fresh mint
Strong coffee black with lemon peel
And roasted watermelon seeds they cracked between their teeth
Only the smell of bitter remains
Only the fear which rises in the acrid east
Only the kafiyeh which roils and reminds in the wind
Only the wound which can not hear the other's wound
The rustle of the other's sacred garments

Having come this far
She can not even stop to take a breath
She bawls like a baby in the desert
She pins the sheets of pain
On her lines and the other's lines
Which now are tangled and confused
torn and intertwined

Can you hear her
She's crying at the checkpoints
She won't take orders easily
She's fumbling for her papers and her pass
At the border she finally proclaims
Her name is wo
And she will not
She will not sharpen perpetual weapons of war
Generations have deemed it so
Not for her father not for her son
Not for this river of red
Which bled
its way through generations of her men
and is bleeding now
She will say amen
She is wo/ she is wo/
Wo wo is woman
Who can hear her who can know
She cries like a sieve in the wind
Having come this far
Who can hear her/who can know

THE HOLINESS GANG

THE HOLINESS GANG

One day a group of angels flies by. They are traveling in a pack and wearing baseball caps acey-deucey which say HOLINESS GANG. "Hey kid," they say, watching me watching them. "Didn't your Ma ever tell you not to mess with the Holiness Gang? Now get going, and next time, keep your bug-eyes to yourself." I look at the ground all the way home, check out the pebbles, the sand, the birthmarks on the small stones, and the dirt; don't look at the flying wiseguys once, and when Ma asks me "What did you today, child?" I focus on the floor, its scars and patterns, and say, "Nothin', I did nothin', ok?"

Then she says, "Well what did you learn today, you must have learned something?" I answer the same. "Nothin'. I learned nothin'. Do you have a problem with that?" She shakes her head. "We just don't seem to talk like we used to," she says. I go into my room and close the door. All I can hear is the flap flap of the wings. All I can see are the baseball caps, poised like a chevron of darkening birds across the blank sky

HOW THE FIGHTS BEGAN

Well the holiness gang gave us lessons
on how to walk and talk and mate and give our precious
gifts away and it always happened
that their words got mixed up with our worlds
and then the fights began
and things got broken and damaged
when they lay that white across the sky
and claimed that white the only game in town
and all the colors sank down in a pile
of wet and stinking feathers
and the rainbow lost its handle
on power and justice and pursuit of happiness
and the colors got lost or sold or snuffed
or old or just plain tired
until at the final
breaking point
the ground became ground/swell
a surge and struggle of colors
meeting east and west and circling north and south
leaning in and leaning out
mountains yielding to the sky
and no one wondering why
no one color better than the rest
and the holiness gang just stood there and gaped
you might say they didn't have a clue
at the Rainbow that was pushing through

ANGEL

Well I really didn't want to approach this one
the huge one the high honcho
the big guy the cell boss of angels the one
I have been leaning/toward/leading /up to/the one
in the corner/the one who swoops/ and flails/and flips
the one who veers/the one who means business
the workaholic one the one
who never goes to Miami the one you knew was in the room
the one I knew was in the room the one who did not leave
the one you tried to smote the one I tried to smote
the one who finally wrapped its wings around you
as you breathed your way into me convulsing
as you flew light and easy as you swarmed
out the window singing *ride ride*
no I am going to leave this
alone I am going
to stop here

singing

ANGEL GHOSTS

I wanted to talk about ghosts
holes in the ground
gates that keep nothing in
windows that knock
doors that are transparent
pictures that fall off the wall
smoke that precedes me up the sacred steps
money that appears and disappears like fools in the fog
crows three of them the persistent black birds
moths that follow me through the pane across the great divide

my father's shovel stuck
up to the hilt in snow
corn cob doll from the flea market
in indiana
sun pennies on the water one in particular
catching the light
bird feeder for chickadees and grosbeak outside
my parents' bedroom window
little bronze boy buried in falling shadow
a cracked stone path leading to an adobe house
saguaro arroyo aieeeee
hare spider red fox
somewhere
angels all angels

PRAISE TO THE GODDESS

Aieeeeeeeeeee
Blooooooooooooooblah tittee bloo blah

All the way to joy street
And back again
A ride
On the great divide
Jammin' that sweet ho up the sacred ladder
That insistent initiator of the mysteries
Steamin' up that fat glad
Good golly ma kali goddess
I saw you
Hummin' that miraculous mother up the stairwell
Hum-jumpin' that sweet tough sister
For dear life and she pullin' you in
For loose strife for daily life for knife
For sword of fire for sword of our desire
For sword of our wonder and our will
For sword of our sumptuous spill
Our emblem and our stain
Our blessed rain
Glad to be home to be whole
Honor her Honor her Honor her
All for dear life
The only life we know

WATER SURROUNDS
THE RED BERRIES

CALL

Black Bird. I all ways
Loved you. Wherever you chose
To fly. Now call home.

The call of the cormorant comes in black ribbon streaks
And cuts into my shoulder blades.
The call becomes a cry of blackness
Calling blackness back from disbelievers

And I am seeking the cormorant still
In creeds and nettles and giant loves
And in the dark time of the night time
I am seeking the cormorant still
To come in a black ribbon streak of light

FOR THE MOUNTAIN

Each day we gallop toward it
Each day we gulp its glacier milk
Each day it molds us into fresh and original creatures
Each day the wind from the Sahara sprinkles rose colored sand on it
Each day we are bleached in its rinsed underpinnings
Each day men kiss its peaks and die on it
Each day it sings down and up dawn and dusk melodies to us
Each day we humble ourselves flat out in front of it
Each day it gives birth to our long chances our relinquished fears
Each day it buries us in its avalanche
Each night we listen to its mewings and cacawings
Its cooings its thunder its rumblings and its utterance
Each night we hear its glowing black repetitions
Why why have we forgotten it
Why have we forsaken each other

Each day it clarifies our hardness
And makes us more tender more simple and more human
Each day we know we can never swallow it though it can swallow us
We can never entirely distance ourselves from it
Though it is our distance
And we laugh as we track its glacial fleas
Each day it throws us out into the new whirl
And we without our tough skin
Our rough stains our sensitive far flung ideas

Each day we arch over and under its overwhelming
Each day we listen to its flip flop birds
Its granite its gneiss and its slate
Its crystal uprisings
Its cold house where rescuers in their helicopters wait at the frozen door
Each day we dread its blank description
And rejoice in its bursts of ruby light
Each day somebody some body is a light in the window
Each day we smell its underside its chalky substance
Each day we mention it forever and truly under our tongues
Each day it does not give us a nod

Each day we are the working body of the work
And the mountain each day we climb
And when we reach the top we fall asleep
We always fall asleep

Each day we dance our devotion like maidens at a festival
And when we stop our mouths are full with mountain stones

BY THE WAY

For Eva and Thomas

First
I went to the hot meadow
With its sunlit grasses
Its warm baked summertime smells
Its city of insects
Where is my friend I asked
And the grasses replied
We haven't heard from him today
He hasn't come by
With his enormous eye
Of kindness
We are his kind by the way
With our tufts and buds and greeny fringes
And our longing toward the sky
But he hasn't been by today
And by the way
We haven't see the dog
either

Then I went to the river
The water was rushing to somewhere
As water has a way of doing
Recovering and churning up
The stones wet and undergoing
I asked them
Where is my friend
They had nothing to say
No news

But look over there
You can see the flat place
Where she lay down
And he moved close
With his insisting eye
Of honesty
Look the grasses are still pressed down
From her spread away spread away ways
And by the way
We haven't seen the dog
either

Then I went to the fire place
I asked for my friend
But I only got a cold response
Empty and void not even a speck of a spark
It couldn't remember
The two shifting figures at dawn
As the light apprehended them
In its relentless approach
Coming over the snow mountains
All rose and glowing
Coming through the shimmering valley
With the glacier milk streaming
My friend close and far away
With his exploring middle eye
Picking up on the flames of continuous licking and leaping
So I asked the cows
Across the way

The brown one the familiar nosed and nudged me gently
She said she had waited all night
In that friendly place near the bench and the fence
The cow remembered how the eye had moved
In her and she too had sighed and moved closer
With her great cow dignity
No sign no sign of our friend the cow chewed and sighed
Digesting her own sorrowful information
Like a patient guru
Swishing her tail in circles
Her teats hanging down toward the dusty earth
And by the way no sign
No sign of the dog
either

So then I went to the jade green alpine pool
Where my friend and I had worked at dusk
Me on the rocks
And he across the way
With his penetrating eye
Catching the last edge of light
Before the dark
As we played out our time together full circle
The tadpoles sashaying here and there
And I asked the wind
Breathing in slow motion circles
Blowing open an old door in my heart
Where something with wings flew out
Into the surrounding night

And the wind in its windy lament said sorry so sorry so sorry
No sign of your friend
And by the way
No sign of the dog
either

SAAS FEE BRIDGE

Crossing the bridge I
leave the burst of fruit the blast
of cold mountain water

Crossing the bridge I greet
the insistence of river . . . mo-
mentum of cow bells

Spilling out and leaping
back . . . rushing past peaks smooth hard
traveling stones speak

Who am I who were
You where will we go what have
You left where we are

WATER

for Mimo Gordon and David Riley

When love tumbles
we know where it lands
in water always in water

Some say love began in water
and water is inside love's silver head

Water is where love returns to
And where it swims out from
each new morning

Water is in love's spring time
its eel grass its salt marsh

In summer water bursts forth
from love's green interior

In autumn water surrounds the red berries
and this is how the lakes begin

In winter it is soundless
water has turned love into hard kernel
some say the beginning of ice

In springtime love begins again
to *yawn and hum /yawn /yawn and hum*

Inside the coves along the bays across the open seas
Love finds its way to water/ and water finds it way to love

SEAWEED

It is the fossil of a fig or a sycamore leaf left after last year's hurricane.
Its edges are folded and torn. It has pock marks.
Its underside is a rough dry sponge.
It is marked and printed with the rubber stamp of a tree.
It is the dried lobe of a small brain. It crinkles. It is allowed one opening, one
salty smell. It is a brown boat for crossing over. Its view threatens my horizon.
When I first came here, I did not know its sound. Its name softened
and sponged me. Its small dots housed armies of miniscule animals.
Nameless hordes. It is a small brown ear.

The ear is listening for the return of my father's first wife, the one who
threw herself off the bridge in our small town. The cry is the cry
he did not cry. The ear knows this and knows that ears are not meant for
crying. That is the business of mouths and noses. But a small brown ear
for crying? Petals of speech break up in laughter. What do ears know? As for
me, I am trying to bring an ear to someone. It is not gathered in or received. It
was the same story with the prayers I used to leave in hollow trees.

ONION

A heavy hand-held burden. Smells
of a million satisfied diners, tufted, sporting
a navel inside out. It's a purse. Mother
of Pearl. A bloated wheel. Rung and ringing, it's
a bell. Full with stinging soup, it's the song's
momma. It's matter. Stung, it's an under-
ground blimp, tissued, filigreed, its packed
oblivion wrapped in belches and huge sighs.

Forgive it. It's pregnant and secret, a tuber baby
banished at birth, a bloated head, tired, tremendous.
Lean into its lemony bag and smell: leftovers from other
suppers, greasy drippings, trimmed covers of old legumes,
a stew to blow on, an uncool pudding, a surprise of skin.
Stripped. Omened. Onioned. Once and for all.

UNDERGOING AND OVERCOMING

Shining elements our tender skin
We become stone later on   sand
We yearn to be covered   led blind
We hurt   open each other up
own what is alive what is dying
what is dead. We mine for love.
For a long time after we are
complete in an awful zinging dread.
Amazing. High noon and no place to go.
Then we make animal sounds. Bird calls.
Vegetal moans. We commence.

shining elements our tender skin tender our elements shining

vegetal moans we commence
then we make animal sounds bird calls
amazing high noon and no place to go
complete in an awful zinging dread
for a long time after we are
what is dead we mine for love
own what is alive what is dying
we hurt open each other up
we yearn to be covered   led blind
we become stone later on sand
shining elements our tender skin

OVERCOMING AND UNDERGOING

We carve our way to the silver hut
where all was lost so long ago
in a place we know. We turn to the bridge
to the cadence to the bead to the thread to the chant
to the chance to bend to the common dance.
Found out we find our way in and in
while all we know is stars are still
above and under the glistening ground
turned round and round by these trembles and shudders
part of what is undergoing and overcoming we stumble about
naked touching grass dirt and root

shining elements our tender skin tender our elements shining

naked touching grass dirt and root
part of what is undergoing and overcoming we stumble about
turned round and round by these trembles and shudders
above and under the glistening ground
while all we know is stars are still
found out we find our way in and in
to the chance to bend to the common dance
to the cadence to the bead to the thread to the chant
in a place we know we turn to the bridge
where all was lost so long ago
we carve our way to the silver hut

ECLIPSE

Driving down east
in the nub- end of fall,
watching the full moon
from my windshield
rise orange and looming
in Kennebunkport,
by Brunswick it was lemon slice
and by Wiscasset it was pale trace
of melon- rind. By the time
I reached Harts Neck Road
in Tenants Harbor
it was eaten out completely,
the nightsky full
with telltale stars.
Wasn't it mute and simple
to stare at each other and kiss,
eat scallops and haddock
then go outside and free the joy/full moon,
restored like Joey, my woeful
unsure third grade poetry student,
writing his way from crescent moon
all the way to full, and then

proclaiming, as if for the first time

I am full
I am full

O slowly now
O slow and easy now

Lick me down
the long and hungry season
of our love

IN THE ALCOVE OF THE HEART

In the tabernacle of the head
In the great ghost factory
   of lung
In the avenue of sight
 In the drum of the ear
   In the omphalos close
     Button and bell
    Warm bake of sex
    In palm and arch
      In ocean wake of touch
       In the wild green tip
       of opening
          The small star
         at the base of the spine
        ducks in and out of caves
       pumps into muscles and veins
      slides into dragon of throat
     announces nipple
    kicks itself into a run
   under the tongue
  begins to sing
   a sound
    at last!

THE RED THREAD

Once there was a lion
Inside a lioness
Once there was a root
Inside a heart
Once there was a rose
In the belly of the thorn
Once there was a father
Inside music
Once there was a pool
Inside a mother
Once there was a garden
Inside a child
Once there was a home
Inside a fire
Now there is a land
Which holds
My heart open
My broken teeth exposed

FAMILY SECRETS

Door of memory opens. Bright green splashes in front of first red house.1762
it says on the door. Blinding sunlight. Shiny laurel leaves. Horse chestnut tree.
At night my father's red velvet smoking jacket. Wine red velvet with black
lapels. Fireplaces in every room. I could jump in and dry out. Die out. Amos
our cocker spaniel his blood running down the road that leads to the IGA.
Mr. Bronson from the market ran over him in the truck and beyond all the
way down to the swan pond. Refugees from Poland in the millhouse. Old Mrs.
Jenner our kindergarten teacher in the dark rooms above the IGA. My ma's
shop The Wool Corner. Miss Porter girls with white men's shirts over their
kilts. Fuzzy brown and black caterpillars crossing the sidewalks. Babysitter
talk above me. Always above me. Yes but. Daddy goes to air raid meetings. Jen
my big sister puts on cape and special cap and makes a victory garden. All
this has happened so long ago. The doll's cracked face. I tried to feed her. The
onion. Peel the onion peel the onion down and down till there is nothing left.

Only the nubbin only the silver tears. Baby sister down the hallway. I was sent
away when the baby came. An old story. Old. My mother is saying to us your
father was married before. Oh. His wife died. How did she die years later the
question asked. She committed suicide drowned herself in the river. Oh. My
father went to identify her. He went with his best friends Bessie and Bucky.
Bessie was Ann's best friend. Ann was in the river. Bessie's daughter was my
best friend. All this happened so long ago. Before me. Before my sisters. Before
my mother. They found her in the Farmington river.
She jumped off the bridge.

Aunt Bessie in the nursing home in Wisconsin said Ann slid into the river near the college highway. They found her handkerchief with her initials. In the trees near the bathhouse. Oh. She was on her way to see Bessie and Bucky but Bessie and Bucky were getting married and my father was best man. At the bridal dinner he received word that his wife was missing. He went home she was gone he never saw her alive again. People in town left lights on their porches hoping she would come home safe. The night she disappeared Police Officer Miller saw her at the crossroads. He said good evening Mrs. Gordon. Where are you going on such a beautiful evening? Taking a walk to the river she said. It was a soft spring evening blossoms popping everywhere. Lime green leaves. Secrets there are always secrets staining the ground of our understanding to keep us grounded.

She had spells. On her trip to Europe she had spells when she got so sad it was like a veil came down on her. Even though she was smart and beautiful. She went to Smith College like Aunt Bessie. My Ma did not go to college. Only money for the boys to go to college. Ann Booth was young when she died. Three years before I was born. For me she was always the woman on the bridge. Faraway. Inaccessible. My sisters thought they were that little baby that lived. Who was I? I was on the bridge waving. Faraway. Inaccessible. Half sister. Our sister. Never talked about. As if she didn't exist. No mention. I was the woman on the bridge. Waving something red. There was a baby born not right. She lived with a woman in town when Ann was in the hospital. First Ann died. A year later the baby died. They never told Ann the truth. They didn't tell her something was different with the baby. Mongoloid they said. Then Down's Syndrome. Our sister. Our half sister. But why wouldn't they let her see the baby? Why did they keep the baby from her? Why was the veil beginning to come down on her? Owning her. Drowning her.

My sister and I, we jump on the beds. We can not stop jumping. Every chance we get we jump on the beds. Sometimes we do somersaults hanging onto the dark posts. I can watch my sister jump. She can watch me. We jump on the beds until we fall down and go to sleep, until the song and prayer comes *jesus tender shepherd hear me bless my little lamb tonight through the darkness be thou near me keep me safe till morning light god bless mommy and daddy and jenny and betty and mimo and gagie and aunt elizabetha and all my friends and relations and make me a good girl for jesus sake amen* and then I really get down to praying please may it go quickly so I can wake up again please let me close my eyes and let it be morning please let me fall away and not remember the dark giant made of shadows who lives in my night who reaches for me from under the bed, and then I try to run and my legs churn and then I try to yell and my screams do not come, my screams are empty bubbles without sound and he reaches me and holds me in his arms down that long corridor, and then the magic comes and saves me the morning comes like magic like the coke I leave under a tree and come back later and I know it has gotten bigger I have a secret a magic secret red thread I don't tell and then I wake up and soon I see my sister's dark braids on the pillow next to me red and later we are jumping up and down on the bedspread red thread the knobs of cloth under my feet, my sister's hair flying up and down we are both jumping the new baby's down the hall and outside the day which will not end floods.

Between two sisters
 I learned at an early age
To use my elbows

BABY SISTER

You were the last extravagance
Of the old man's seed.
You were too blond
For me
And I was dark
And deeply rest-
Less. I wanted you
To stop.
And when you didn't
I held the rage
Between my scabby knees
For years. Still
I wanted to hold
You.
Ma said when you were born
I'd let you drop.
They sent me away.
When I came home
I couldn't hold
On anything.
Numbers or colors or even
Cutting paper. I learned
To stutter.
What did you expect?
A song?
Forget it.
I am almost old.
I want to hold you.

MUSIC

I wanted to talk about
music the lack of it
in our new england house
on old mountain road
the house
my ma called
the catbird seat
the place with the medium-
sized rocks except for that huge boulder
my old man buried when we moved in
there was simply so little
music a burl ives 78 which had blue tail
fly sweet betsy from pike
my handsome winsome johnny
and my favorite cotton eyed joe.
another record casey would waltz
with the strawberry blond
and the songs ma sang to us like baby boats of silver
blue did you ever go a fishin' on a rainy rainy day
and my dad's old college song born on the steps of durphy
and in kindergarten we sang blue birdy
blue birdy through my window and little purple astor
on the yellow school bus they sang
pistol packin' mama
certainly no jazz though my best friend jane could play kitten
on the keys and at school we sang stouthearted men and night and day
and I had swan lake to dance to and nutcracker
still there was little music

it wasn't part
of our home mostly it was quiet
after dinner reading or stories and homework
upstairs fights and fusses at the dinner table
arguments discussions my mother saying to herself delectable if i do say so
myself or the scary times when my father
threatened to pack his bags or when the voices got loud in the livingroom i
didn't want a thunderstorm or an outburst
i hoped for a long laugh to limber
up the rafters but not the one gin too many loud sound
most times it was quiet after dinner reading
but little music
later on we had 45s shows musicals we loved south pacific oklahoma
showboat we went to square dances dosey doed our partners we went to
dancing school and learned how to foxtrot and dip
do the conversation i remember rosemary clooney and tennessee waltz
my father's favorite was who stole my heart away
so i guess there was always a little music
that summer i was thirteen in cuttyhunk beautiful
beautiful brown eyes and i was born to wander i was born to roam but mr and
mrs sippi made me feel at home but still we had so little music when gordon
came home from the war we sang hubba hubba ding ding baby you got
everything and he taught us flat foot floozy with a floyfloy.

Lay that pistol down babe lay that pistol down.

SPLIT FOR LOVE

I am 13. He is 13.
We are on an island in summer
with no home but our hearts.
I am Betty Gordon. He is Stetson Drake.
Cuttyhunk's the place
A chunk of land
In the Cape's bright flow.
For five days in August
after going to the dock
to see if the sword fish have come home
bloodied and done for
we play a game with a knife called
Split.

We face each other
legs closed and obedient.
We take the knife in turns.
First me. Then him. Then him. Then me.
Holding the blade in one hand
I flip the knife diagonally and aim close but not
too close to the opposite foot of my friend.
If the knife does not enter the waiting turf, if it lies flat on the summer grass,
the girl loses her turn. Now it's up to him. He holds the blade.
He aims near but not too near. The girl moves her foot to where
the knife is up to the hilt in dirt.
Wide and wider turn after turn we go
until one of us can stretch no further.
Then the other wins:
Split.

We begin again.
Split.
This hot game throughout the splash
Of August ages us quick as heat.
On Labor Day we take the last walk to the ferry
Together.

The boy takes the girl's hand.
Everyone notices. She quakes in all the places
Where the knife does not pierce
Where the blood begins
A slow pulsing song
Forever.
In September after school starts
The first letter arrives.
On the outside in black crayon is drawn
A lock and key
It is addressed to Mrs. Stetson Drake.
Everyone sees:

My older sister will not let this letter
Stained by love
Disappear and die.

Dear Betty,
Last night I played canasta with my parents, and all the while I thaw of you. I grew
1 and ½ inches while I was down Cuttyhunk. Now I am 5 Feet 5 and ¾ inches tall.
If you like or love me as a boyfriend, you can keep my picture. But if you hate or
dislike me, please send it back. I love you. Sincerely Stetson Drake.

The dye begins
And spreads its shape
Wide and wider
Out and over
Till the knife can go
No further
Or no deeper
And the two become
One
Split
Split for love

LISTENING IN ON ETH
An Evocation: for Etheridge Knight

Woke up full of mississippi
the far cries. the farm. mama's animals cows pigs chickens rabbits
bitin' snakes intertwined uncle cat eye
hosie rosie aunt dink uncle pink my cousins miss lilac lips
the old cars men always underneath 'em.
shotgun house. railroad flat. rat titty chasing big sis
clear through the rooms one after another and out
the far end. outdoor toilet.
doves. scratchgrass in the moonlight.
possum and coon. snakes in the red dust. you ain't better'n
nobody else and nobody better'n you. mama—teachin'.
charles. floydell. me. clyneese. honey. dale. janice.
a stingin' in the blood as I walk along the road.
goin home with the song singin' in the blood.
mine flowin' out. stingin'
on the road between here and paducah and further.
always further
charles drove me to the city limits dropped me off
do you really want to go junior he asks?
take a train to chicago. kansas city too. see, see rider, see what you done done.
red dust taste. it's the soup we sing on.
neckbones and collard greens
ol' hound mouth. learned the songs from him out on the streets in the parks
said them over and over. over and over.
never did subscribe to no rules. like be home by dark.
let the good times roll. down home. runnin' with the wild ones.
bleedin'. hurtin' too. how should i have known.
the hole. the dry shave. the baseball bat.
head cracked open like a ripe melon.
no women to look to for comfort.
just the steel doors clangin' shut keys lockin' us in.
maybe the guys from pendleton were right.

72

i am a low rider. c c rider. see what you done done.
outside the nickel in those last days. slidin' down the walls
on the hot nights when e was back in beantown
an ol' mr. k bottoming out
fulla dark eyes and ol' man death close up on my neck hairs
my heart fulla desperation
fear of cessation and a lil' bit
of wonder. one two. buckle my sorry ass shoe
nobody's lookin' round now
'cept ol joe and fishface
down town and six feet under you think it was a party e
when you first went to michigan city
asked about a prison wood shop like the one in thomaston maine
on the way to tenants harbor carved boats shiny polished boxes
rockin' chairs remember we are movin' closer
in up and around between beyond whichever way we turn
you'll find me dawgin' you.... i told you so

Etheridge Knight, African-American poet (1931-1991) was born in Corinth, Mississippi and later moved with his family to Paducah, Kentucky, and then Indianapolis, Indiana. He left school in eighth grade, ran away from home three times, joined the army underage, and got hooked on drugs in his twenties and spent most of his thirties in county jails and, finally, the state penitentiary at Michigan City, Indiana. He was in prison when he first started to write and read his poems, and where his first poems were published with Broadside Press in Detroit. EK went on to become one of America's most engaging and powerful poets, and he was considered to be a master practitioner of the Oral Tradition. He was the author's friend and companion during the last decade of his life. She was with him till his death in Indianapolis in March 1991, where they lived in a public housing apartment at 555 Massachusets Avenue, referred to by Etheridge as 'The Nickel.'

FISH

forEtheridge Knight

When you first arrived
at Indiana State Penitentiary
Michigan City
that's what you were
fish
you had that fresh/fish smell
you had that fresh/fish look
and you had to watch your fresh/fish back
and when the others came up from Pendleton
the young militant blacks
and you watched
and rejoiced
that's what they were
fish
but a new and dangerous breed
voicing Revolution
by that time
you were in love with fish
you had your own tank
in your cell
and you fell *in love* with fish
In the beginning you had the tank for the light
so you could read your way deep
into the night and sink solitary
and reckless into fanon
and malcolm and aj rogers and haki
langston and sonia and gwen and dudley
bly and louis un/te/meyer's an/thol/og/y of modern po/e/try
the title said so slowly and deliberately
you could taste the syllables

and later you fell in love with the fish
You liked to watch them swirl and glide
and sometimes when you were casting out of the pen
and angling for a flip/tail swish of a thought
you would open up your prison/vision to the fish
and you knew you were in love
in love with the scent and the ink
in love with the fish
nosing their way up against
the common glass

DOWN HOME BALI STYLE

I thought of you in Paducah Kentucky
At twelve pitching pennies/playing pool
Dealing cards/shooting craps
You wanted to be like George Raft
But this is end of day in Penestanan Village Bali
Guys pull up on motorbikes
Home from the ricefields and the tourist hotels
They hang up their helmets move quickly into inner sanctum
Under shade tree/near stone wall of family compound
(nearly sixty people live here)
Women back/further with the children/prepare food/string beads
Make offerings/exchange news/ grandmother dadong with bare flat breasts
Hums and prevails/kids home from river bathing with their mothers
Run naked through the dusklight/men slide ruppiahs ceremoniously
Out from pressed centerfolds of their sarongs/ten percent of winnings
Goes to village/this year they are building a new tower for the kulkul bell
The closing of the circle/the young bloods stand tight with pony
Tails and Dallas cowboy tees/with fanny packs and tattoos/
The elders squat up on the bank/suck on clove cigarettes/
New babies are held high on hips of young fathers/
The red sun bleeds down the sky/ the razor-sharp four inch
Stiletto knives in the sleek packets are inspected/compared/ argued over
Decided upon/ tied to the cock's leg with green and orange string

Then the preening/the stroking/ the signifying/
the braggadocio/the kissing of the beak/the comb/
the prying open of the eyes/the peering under the wings/ the oil on the knife/
special oil holy oil/ that makes the cooking sweeter/
the whispering of blessings/ the throwing of the cocks into the ring/ the sudden
flurry/outburst/rustle of feathers/ flame of violence/
no decision/cover them with the bamboo basket/
uncover the fight till death
the hush/the gasp/ the cut/ the twitch
the quick demise/drops of blood
like rasp/berries in the dirt
inspection under the wing
the drag of the dead bird home to the victor's soup pot
the paying up/ the paying out/ disbanding of the band/ the bond still tight
till tomorrow night/ same place
till death us do part

we really love this game

THE RED THREAD

Imagine trudging these slushy roads this crunched winter February stormday, the storm subsiding the sun riding us up Pearl Street down Mass. Avenue past the Cambridge Bicycle Shop past the bewitched female mannequins we name Saraswati and Isis past the sullen male mannequin in the next block half clad half hidden his hand slipped into a private swath of cloth, and we decide he's about to spring the drugstore window and surprise the suddenly writhing goddesses down the street. Past the New England Confection Company building with the turret of giant pastel NECCO wafers, past the stone sweep of M.I. T.; we traverse the pepper pot bridge, past the multi layered pedestrians with their frisky dalmatian, and out of the blue you ask me about death.

Death? Death. And no you aren't so much interested in the process of dying, of course you could predict I wouldn't want any emergency situation, no extraordinary measures nothing like that, just a simple lean into the wind surrounded at times by my only daughter my sonny boy my grandchildren my two sisters and their men, my abiding friend, Judith, my mother and father and Etheridge though dead for a decade startlingly alive for the passage. I propose chants and some poems, a pillow to windward, no voluptuary esoteric practices no howls and lamentations, no sharp salt keenings, no arch into spillage, no carbonization of tears whelmed and overwhelming; simply you holding a golf ball and a carved wooden statue of baby girl jesus or the blissful buddha boy, our hands searching for some felt finality, a goodbye at twilight before the gateless gate. No you say, keep it simple. I want to know what you feel about *after*.

After? Well who can know what happens after. But I guess I think we are all connected up, part of something else, communication running on not running out, no end to this beginning. *What?* you say, I can't hear you my ears covered with my hat and my hood and then the traffic from Storrow Drive. *Red Thread* I say. It's like the *Red Thread*. That's helpful, you say turning toward me with the full thrust and attention of your whole body.

And just at this weathering moment on this snow feathery winter path leading
us to the downtown crossroads, near all the monochromatic winter scene,
the bend back bushes, the fragile bridges, the agile guides, the low lying tree
trunks with curving cross branches, near the well protected parka people, just
at this moment out of almost nowhere in the middle of the path appears a red
thread a bright red ribbon curved and sinuous spread out in front of us seconds
after I have said after death
　　the messages continue, messages ribboning here and beyond the conscious
expanding
　　　out from the body's borders into the landscape of our love and longing,
look you say
　　　　　someone's left a red leash on the path, no I say it's not a leash
　　　　　　　look it's a *red thread* wending its way kneading us into something like
　　needing us not wanting us no you say not needing us just on the path
　　　you can't overlook it the city around us the synchronicity what can we say
when it is so powerfully red thread smack in front of us unfurled on this path
this *red thread* like
15ᵗʰ century zen crazy ikkyu, like emily d's sequestered amherst passion, like
our mutual friend colorado ed's dharma trajectory from here to here . . . here
like our own hands searching each other awake out of the long curve of red
　　ribbon the runway we have landed on which will follow us still further
when we move to a place we can not see this long ribbon moving ahead of us
　　　　　uncoiled like a snake roiled and ribboning
　　　through time and season sensuous and sensual
　　　　　ribboning us awake *red threading* us

　　　　　　　to what came before and what will come. After.

BEE HOLDING

BEE HOLDING

Saw a bee fly by my head
  it was burning
Heard my own small girl
  swallowing the sunlight
she was humming
  Lately I've been turning
to the ringing
  through the window
Today outside the springtime
  I almost tasted snow
We were frozen splinters once
There's a bee above my head
  It's calling riding
Had a lover once
  And never told my husband
Saw his face above my bed
Heard a bell inside my head

Lately/ I've been/dying
  for the honey/in the stinging

2.
I held it in my hand.
It didn't sting or fly away
In fact it stayed
through all that season
till the weather swarmed
 and changed.
I didn't know
what it could mean
or why I cried

3.
Outside our door a brogue of bees astir in the honey
till dark when the wind shoves through unhinges the cage
turns pale deposits me out of bounds where animals run
their eyes alive with fright. I come to find the fire.
I follow the humming to the bush. Nothing is left.
I run to the witching stones the land bleeds dry
I reach for the sky the sky scoops me up
spits me back I splinter in blades
of grass I lie through my teeth
when I tell honey
bees I like
to lie in the sun
a bush in the sun in the heat alive with bees.

4.
There are bees in sarajevo bees
in baghdad in chicago and soweto there are
bees in santiago there are bees in belfast
there are bees in bosnia there
are bees in boston as we speak
there are bees in rwanda there are bees in congo
bees in colorado there are bees
in bethlehem there are bees
in haiti bees in afghanistan bees in bali
bees in paris in jerusalem in new york
bees on their way to me
yes to you

It's not a secret anymore

AT A CERTAIN MOMENT BY NO ONE'S CLOCK

For Paolo Knill

The child can not yet tell time
The scarlet bird stops its innocent play
And turns without warning into the city's
Bomb what can the child do but scream
But hide inside the silver hut where
He sees out where no one sees in
Where the dream is a dream of petals
Flying off of blood in the gutter of out-
Raged birds and nests of mothers hunting
For recognizable remnants among rubble

Of the body the human body doing
A charred unnatural dance

FIRE

Flames insist their way
into the most minimal
passageways.

Nothing here is at rest.
Everything leaps and breathes
with some other dancing self.

Yes. Many have died here
Some didn't come back. Some did.
It was a question of the heat's intensity.
And timing

At one point
the flames took over
everything. There was no going
anywhere but
Red.

The animals baffled were led from the barn.
The birds in terror fled from the forest.
All I remembered
afterward was the soft
touch of ash. Where there had
been land. Where the trees had sighed
and produced fruit.

Bonfires every-
where. And the small
sounds of birds gasping
uncommonly. In the common

smoke.

SMOKE

My smoke
is in your fire

Your fire
is in my forest

My forest
is on your land

Your land
is on my boundary

My boundary
is on your frontier

Your frontier
is on my shoreline

My shoreline
is in your water

My water is on your mountain
Your mountain is on my Sahara

My Sahara is in your wind
Your wind is in my breath

Your breath is in my song my song is in your
story your story is in my heart my heart is your hands your
hands are on my body my body
is on your mind your
mind is in my spirit
my spirit is in your fire your fire
is in my life my life

My life!
My life is on fire!

WHEN I HOLD YOU DYING

I learn

that breathing *in*
is a kind of birth into
the body
and breathing out
is a birth
into the uni/verse
the one verse
a continuous rhythm
in and out
in/in and out

I hold you from behind
with my arms around you
my hands on your heart
You birth into me
as you die
and
I live into you
as you birth into death
your weight finally flopping like a fish into my arms
your breath growing light and lighter still
we are in the shallows now
as you leave the water
as you make your way to the faraway country

your gasps and convulsions
moving into me
rhythmically
as I breathe into you
and you breathe out
into the big sea of silence

where I can not follow

SANTA ANA CANYON

We know now
That everything is gone
Except each other and the animals.
All the rest has disappeared
In the insistent sieve of the wind
We hold each other and weep.
We weep as if someone else
Is holding us we weep
And ghosts of our possessions
Float away through the charred air
From the Santa Ana canyon
Through all its dominions.
But wait. The young daughter
Has found a small memento:
A ceramic pot she made.
What is contained?
Again the whole family holds
Each other and weeps. The sounds
Of our weeping surge on the up-
Draft and veer through the vast hands
Of the Santa Ana Canyon.
Ana Canyon
Canyon

.

IT WAS ON THE ROOF THEY SAY
THE EDGE OF THE ROOF

It loved the hurricane
  It swam the waterways
    It loved the sun they say
      It felt the snow they say

  It went away they say
    They never heard from it again they say
      They never wanted it/or its issue/ its mother/ its friends
      They never saw it moving through

flames/the passage of seasons/birth/the mating cries
  They were getting on in the world with lives of their own
    Substantial lives/ they lived beneath a tower/ they had insurance
    They had the data/ they had the memo/ they had the fax

So after it went away they refused to think about it
  But sometimes at night when the air is difficult to breathe
    They hear a rustling in the room and they know
    They don't want to know but they know

And their fingers search for each other like they're searching for the buried keys
  And their eyes close like shutters in a hurricane
  And when they dream they see it and they see it and they see. . . .

EVENING RAGA

The windows I look toward still
are *faraway*, everything is *far-*
away and still, everything

shares with my beloved, *faraway*,
faraway he has taken my speech, still
what more can I say to him

he who has taken my speech, he who
first taught me how to see, he who
told me never to be afraid.

There are things in this world which shall never be mine,
which shall always move through me .
Let's not say what this is and what it isn't.
It is too big for that and too small.

It is evening.
Light falls away from the city
and now I look for him on the paths beyond the towers.

LANGUAGE

The tongue wakes
in the heat of its hunger
Power is
everywhere
and all I want to say
is said simply
as if I am a child

Ladybug Ladybug flyaway home
Your house is on fire your children are gone

I swing out into a clearing
I do not smile
but I am pleased
as I repeat the words

All but one and her name is Anne
and she crept under the fryin' pan

I fear
I love you
I fear
I may die soon
I want you
to love me

love/you/love/me

QUESTIONS

Why the wings in the middle of your chest
Why the throat like a bridge
Why the magpies flying over the freeway
Why the flap of the crow's wings
On the pane of my mother's last room
Why cars crossing over crossing back
Why the bloody trail of roadkill
Why the township of heart
Why the well at the crossroads
Why the whirligig of belly
Why this tuneful beginning
Why the sudden flood at noon
Why the ice on the puddle
Why the runes on the frozen stone
Why the mud and the muddle
Why the friend who is dying of aids
Why the love messages on the blue screen

Let the wild horse stay
Let the work horse go
Let the wild horse go
Let the work horse stay

Hold on
Let go

All the same
Dance the dance
Of pleasure pain

ALLOWING THE DANCE

CRACKING

It's hard to remember my own cracking
And how I asked for pictures more pictures
Suddenly I felt appetite
I knew I was a singing creature among many
My spine was released by bells
I experienced melting and multiplying
When you came I couldn't remember your name
Though you had filled my dreams
The windows were knocking
The doors became transparent
Light poured through
The amazed fish joined and jumped
There was somebody playing the tuba
At which point the whole damn high school band joined in
A chorus of frogs up and offered themselves out of ponds
And in a place I could only know
With the soles of my feet
I up and started to dance
And you
danced and you
danced and you danced and you
And you danced and you danced and you danced and you
and we all danced
Into the new season
Which was suddenly
Ours!

MOON DOG SONG

Moon dog's back in town
today a giant of a dog
splashing down the hill
licking everything in
sight. I can't believe
how big he seems,
heaped in his own shadow
over-taking it
and stretching me
more than before.
We leap
and know where we are
reaching
om o mo oh mo om mo om
as mo dog undergoes me over-
takes me wide and deep
again and once again
we lurch
up the hot and sacred stairs
and up and up
we search
the steep ecstatic skies
and up and up and up
we yelp toward gods and dogs for help
for a place we knew
was in us
all the time

SOMEWHERE

there will be a reason
for me
to go down on you
somewhere in all the weathers
to come
coaxing the sweet reed
to seed cooing gently
to my body-
guard and long lost pal
my ramblin' man
my wand
my under/stander
my
plunderer
thunderer
mister
sting song
singalong
my come now
my give it
up man
my golden rod
my guide
across and through
my window
my tree outside
is swaying as I write
she taps
(that's the boy in her)
she sways
(and that's the girl)

ALL IN ALL

In/spired on your root
I spiral down and around
as steam heat abounds

We rise high and sink
deep in surrounding hot springs
follow spice route home.

ALLOWING THE DANCE

for Norma Canner

We crawl on hands and knees to the center of heat
   to the center of our bodies:
      the ghettos, the hot enclaves, the hidden suburbs
        with uncut grasses, the barrios at midnight.

We curve ourselves round what we hold in the soft center,
   in the moist beginning, we learn what we hold and curve
      over as children, and I am back in the small green place
        combing, combing for sound.

I begin to touch lumps of it:
   the rough barky surface, the black intensity, the white pain
      where no one is protected, the heart of the red
        clay matter where we chew. We learn of this space

and how we must breathe with it, our bodies
   move slowly out from that space into the new, we learn
      when it is time to move, moving to the slight gesture
        of each fingertip, of each nail, the fronts and backs

of hands, of genitals, we learn what the toes hold,
   we begin to move with the animals, whole bands and tribes
      of them moving in tandem. We move, we stretch toward what
        we want, we stay as long as we need to, we don't leave

until it is time to leave, we breathe deeply, we whistle, we roll
    into an old toy, a drum, a leaf, a stringed instrument
        on which we play an old song. We ponder the new song
            we know in the soft center we don't have to leave,
                to crumble, we don't have to throw something away

before we begin to name it, we sing to it
    it sings back to us, we listen for it, it begins to grow,
        we wait for it, we wish on it, we begin to appear
            we roll across dreams like children in meadows

we roll on our bellies, our bellies say we have waited long enough.
    We can not be appeased, we ring out with the salt tides of rage,
        the sweet lullabies, the prayers, we fling ourselves outdoors,

we pursue our hunger down back alleys, we don't stop
    until we are ready to stop, we heave ourselves down on rocks, we
        search for breath, we sleep, we careen into our skins, into
            the heat we were born into where we slap our sides, pry open
                our eyelids, where we make animal sounds, *we talk.*

Now we are moving together, now we are animals moving together
    into our dread, into the beauty of our skins, our weight,
        our textures. We clump across plains, pushing aside

huge promises which never finally licked us, which obscured
    our vision. We paste wild calls on our bodies, our fingers ache
        to see. Our ears run ahead of sound, we remember the strangers
            we were and we plow the strangeness down. We move
                into space like children beginning

PLEASE COME TO MY BIRTHDAY PARTY
I NEED YOU

Afraid
of spilling over spilling out beside the point-
pointless unfocused blurry lost skidding going down
the hill too fast and me with no way to stop
to consider the mindful approach
wha wha wha all the way home
blurting blabbering stuttering finally getting
to the uttering being rung stood in a corner supposedly
concealed at sixty years old ha ha finally
revealed reveling by the river unraveling
mississippi ayung charles rivermaid seine of the old town st george ma ganga
where are my lovers where is my only girl where is my sonny boy
where are my friends till the end compañera compañero
will you never forsake me will you always laugh at my jokes
will you take my hand in the strange dark
when I bump into undiscovered objects on my way to the sea
where is my father in all this my talent
where is my sack of poems where are my ratchety songs
where is the ballad that steals my heart
where the hell is my heart
and where is my ma when I need her
where is the crow that tapped on her window
where are my sisters who stand beside me
where are my brothers in all this clutter where is my mask and my act
where is the bridge and the edge where is elizabetheridge
where is the badge and the ridge
Can we begin to continue our ending all over again
Isn't it time to have a party
Isn't it time to laugh

SUMMER DRIFT

Blue gold smear of days
We discuss nothing with gulls
Grow inward and calm

Dreams slap in and out
Between the black scales of night
Strong necks drag huge fish

Beach hibiscus pulse
Frail tissues in summer wind
Water laps returns

HOUSE EARTH WATER SKY

CONTENT

To have
a room
to go to:
To look
out the window
and down
the street:
To watch
leaves turn:
to begin with them
and breathe deep
into their fall
to earth:
To have a sill
with a jar full
of mums
and marigolds:
To have a shell
from the ocean
with a deep mysterious
pink inside:
All this
in one room!

THE HEAVY OBJECT

Many times I heard the voice
Of the heavy object:
Behind closed doors
Through small holes
Across frontiers at dawn

Many times I was too tired to meet
The heavy object
Much less to move it
At those times I stopped
Wanting a cool forest
Its resting places
My legs were too tired to carry me
And I slept
Balancing small perfect circles
On the outside edge of my dreams

I turned and turned with the heavy object
Until it became green and manageable
Until we could call each other by our real names
Until we could dance with each other
Until we could hold each other and weep
Until we could regain what we knew as children
A real bird a mountain a snail all coral in the shape
Of a realizable mountain a circle above another circle
Below and three roads leading to the sky
And the sky completely empty of any object
Completely free

THIRTEENTH SEASON OF THE OLD CRONE

Out of the giant hole
   Into the gasp of air
      The thrust and chant of morning

Into the smudge of stars
   The canopy of splinters
      In time with the bear

With the muskrat
   The staggering plants
      The old crone crawls out from under

With winter as an incidental she has come through

With water surrounding her hands
   In the light of the spring and its high
      Pitched cries she has come through

She has come through
   Onto a meadow of ice where flowers melt
      And burn she has come through

Where children move enchanted
   Into the promise of monsoon
      Where beasts befriend her nuzzling and wet

She walks where she must this long condition of flight

Where birds with beaks like stilettos
   Aim their chevrons carefully
      Where she marks time with migrations

Where every night she dips on her hands and knees

 Disappears into throats and nets
    Scratches for snow and goldfish
       Dips into the silt of caves

She is moved by the motions of insects
   Their cries their matings
      Praying mantises eating each other's limbs

She looks for the moth and its shifting powders
   The stillness of stones in the drone of heat
      She listens to the voices of relatives

Folded between the listless sleep of fossils
   Traces the patterns of their careers their crimes
      She turns with the moon and its silver scars

HOUSE EARTH WATER SKY

The heart
Of the matter
Rests
On the roof of the sky
We only go by
We only go by

And what is unfinished
Is always unfinished
And what is finished begins again

And the green goes over and over

And now
As a child holds
A night time lullaby
We all become a part of loving

The sound belongs to the silence
The silence belongs to the sound
The dark earth belongs to the sunlight
The sunlight belongs to the ground

And the green goes over and over

Give
The love
The lasting pleasure
Give it
In full measure
Find the fruit
Be at the special spot
Beat the drum
Be here
Be there
Again and once again
Bear it Wear it We are it
What else have we got
We do We do We do
Desire
it

We are scared and sacred
We are scared and sacred
We are scared and sacred
In the hoop of the world
And the green goes over and over

ON THE EDGE

If you fall here you
Fall into another world
So pay attention

An agile guide's good
When you cross a fragile bridge
From here . . . to here . . . here

To walk on the edge
You must follow your faithful
Feet and not look down

What can I tell you?
Where I'm from? How I escaped?
Wild sky glimpsed through leaves!

UPRISING

You do not will
what emerges

what emerges
will teach you
You only must be ready
to receive the messages
and the messages
are everywhere

song
up-lifting
off the leaves
of trees

the effortless encounter
with the universe

Remarks

Most of these poems were made over the past twelve years. Some arrived through work with my partner in performance, Paolo Knill; some through drawing in journals, words interwoven with colors, textures, and shadings; some through moving with others in community dance; some through working in ensemble with musicians and poets; others through photographs and their black and white Xeroxes trailing strands of red; some poems were inspired by letters revealing the tell/tale journeys we take each day; many poems arrived through the decade lived close to Black American Poet Man Knight; some through abiding friends and familiars, students and colleagues, lovers and dear ones; other poems were inspired by listening to the voices of children as I do regularly; some poems came to me from the rise and the fall of the winds and tides, from taking the heat, from being left out in the cold, from random choices, premeditated decisions and lucky mistakes, from the counterpoint of resistance and invitation, from nothing on my mind into something in my poems. Red Thread!

My friend, Ed Werner, in Colorado sent me a copy of Crow With No Mouth versions by Stephen Berg of writing by IKKYU, 15th century renegade Zen poet who referred to the red thread. I began to find red traces everywhere, this lively ribbon pulling me back and pushing me forward. As I began to visualize and gather poems for this book, the red thread appeared and disappeared into reverie, on alert, into revelry, into undercover smudge, into an enormous apron in a wide sky, into bramble, into brash emblem and bright graffiti, into crumpled cloth on dream pillow, into the sift and weave of early childhood and old age, somewhere out from the private middle of things into public space, red thread caught in the updraft, a sudden gust across the Sahara in a big wind and poured onto glacier, a crimson trajectory, a curl of the Atlantic, the rim of the Pacific, onto ma ganga, into conflagration and incendiary, across border and checkpoint and always held by and holding onto a constant tribe of extended family and friends, my two sisters and their husbands and children, my daughter my sonny boy my granddaughter human beings waving red threads from bridges, their beloved voices reaching me in the circulating air. And don't forget those who appear: *After.*

And Marge Piercy my editor: writer and poet my friend over years
And Ira Wood writer publisher and friend
  these two who saw me through
  and all those who see me through

A profound thank you.

About the Author

Elizabeth Gordon McKim is a poet whose roots are in the oral tradition of song, story, and chant. She reads, performs, and teaches in the United States and internationally. Known for four previous books of poetry: *Burning Through*, *Body India*, *Family Salt*, and *Boat of the Dream*, she has published in some of the nation's most engaging magazines, including *Poetry*, *Poiesis* (Canada), *Ploughshares*, *River Styx*, *Painted Bride Quarterly*, *Blue Sofa Review*, *Drumvoices*, and *Epoch*. She has been a visiting poet in hundreds of schools and colleges, and has been the Artist-in Residence for six years at, and in 2003 was named Poet Laureate of, the European Graduate School for Expressive Arts Therapy in Switzerland. She is the co-author with Judith Steinbergh of *Beyond Words: Writing Poems With Children*, a pioneering text which has been in print for more than two decades. She is a member of the National Faculty of Lesley University in the Department of Creative Arts in Learning, and lives in Brookline, Massachusetts.

About the Type

This book is typeset in Minion, a 1990 Adobe Originals typeface by Robert Slimbach. Minion is inspired by classical, old style typefaces of the late Renaissance, a period of elegant, beautiful, and highly readable type designs. Created primarily for text setting, Minion combines the aesthetic and functional qualities that make text type highly readable with the versatility of digital technology.

Composed by JTC Imagineering, Santa Maria,CA
Designed by John Taylor-Convery